headwork reading

The Driving Lesson

Chris Culshaw

...ity Press

The Driving Lesson

Julie was seventeen. She was learning to drive. Her uncle Phil was giving her lessons in his car.

One day uncle Phil said, 'Drive down to the market. I must get some flowers for your gran.'

Julie jumped into the car and started the engine. She put on her seat belt and checked her mirror.

When it was safe, she pulled out into the traffic.

'Very good,' said her uncle, 'but watch your speed. This isn't a race. Look out for that girl on the bike.'

'I can see her, uncle.'

'Yes, but has she seen you? Give her plenty of room when you overtake.'

'Do you think I'll pass my test, uncle Phil?' Julie said.

'Don't worry about the test,' he said. 'Keep your eye on that van in front. It's turning right.'

'Yes, uncle Phil. I can see that, uncle Phil.'

'What have I told you?'

'Keep a safe distance between me and the car in front.'

'Very good,' he smiled. 'You are my star pupil.'

They arrived at the market. Julie parked the car. Uncle Phil jumped out. 'You wait here, Julie,' he said. 'I'll be back in a minute.'

Julie watched her uncle walk over to the flower stall. All of a sudden, a boy came racing through the market on a mountain bike. He was wearing a ski mask over his face. When he got to

the flower stall, he stopped. He reached over and grabbed the cash box. Uncle Phil grabbed his jacket.

He tried to pull the boy off the bike but he lost his grip. The boy raced off through the market.

Uncle Phil ran back to the car and jumped in. 'Follow that bike!' he shouted. Julie started the engine and set off.

'Turn right!' shouted her uncle.

Julie turned right. 'Oh dear,' she said. 'This is a bus lane!' There was a big red bus in front and one behind.

'Turn left then. Before we get boxed in!' shouted uncle Phil. Julie turned left.

'Then second right and first left,' he said.

'Are you sure?' said Julie, starting to panic.

'Trust me,' said uncle Phil, 'I used to drive a tank in the Army! It's a short cut.'

'A short cut to where?' gasped Julie. 'Heaven?'

'Very funny,' snapped her uncle. 'Mind that dog!'

Just then Julie saw the boy on the bike again.

'Look,' she said, 'there he is. He's taken his ski mask off. He thinks he's got away with it. He doesn't know we're following him. He hasn't spotted us, has he uncle?'

'No. He thinks he's in the clear.'

The boy stopped next to the post office. He got off his bike and went into a phone box.

'Now's our chance,' said uncle Phil. 'Onto the pavement, Julie.'

'What? But isn't that against the law?'

'Just do as I say. Drive onto the pavement. Slowly.'

Julie drove the car onto the pavement very slowly.

'Mind that old man! Watch out for that dog. Good, that's it. Now... park the front of the car right up against

the phone box. Good. Well done! A very neat bit of driving. You must have had a good teacher.'

The boy in the phone box saw what was happening but it was too late. He was trapped. Uncle Phil grinned at

him, 'I'm not going to let you escape again. Better phone the police, Julie.'

'But how?' asked Julie, pointing to the phone box.

Uncle Phil pulled out his mobile phone. 'I never go anywhere without this. You never know what might happen...'

Julie smiled, 'It's been a great driving lesson.'

Uncle Phil looked at the boy in the phone box, 'Yes, and I think he's learned a lesson too, don't you?'

Oxford University Press, Walton Street, Oxford, OX2 6DP

Oxford New York
Athens Auckland Bangkok Bogota Bombay
Buenos Aires Calcutta Cape Town Dar es Salaam
Delhi Florence Hong Kong Istanbul Karachi
Kuala Lumpur Madras Madrid Melbourne
Mexico City Nairobi Paris Singapore
Taipei Tokyo Toronto Warsaw

and associated companies in
Berlin Ibadan

Oxford is a trade mark of Oxford University Press

© Chris Culshaw 1998
First published 1998

ISBN 0 19 833592 X

Printed in Great Britain

Illustrations by Gary Wing